C000174471

# The Key of Faith

Written and compiled by Sarah M. Hupp

Illustrated by C. James Frazier

Designed by Arlene Greco

INSPIRE

Inspire Books is an imprint of
Peter Pauper Press, Inc.

For permissions please see
the last page of this book.

Text copyright © 1999
Peter Pauper Press, Inc.
202 Mamaroneck Avenue
White Plains, NY 10601
Illustrations copyright © C. James Frazier
Licensed by Wild Apple Licensing
All rights reserved
ISBN 0-88088-127-5
Printed in China
8  7  6  5  4  3

Visit us at www.peterpauper.com

# The Key of Faith

Jesus said:

"If you have faith as small
as a mustard seed, you
can say to this mountain,
'Move from here to there'
and it will move.
Nothing will be impossible
for you."

*Matthew 17:20 NIV*

Now faith is being sure of
what we hope for and certain
of what we do not see.

*Hebrews 11:1 NIV*

Sometimes, faith is

not clinging;

faith is letting go.

*Glenn Van Ekeren*

Faith is the sturdiest, the most
manly of the virtues . . .
It is the virtue of the storm,
just as happiness is the
virtue of the sunshine.

**Ruth Benedict**

Active faith gives thanks
for a promise, even though it is
not yet performed; knowing
that God's contracts are
as good as cash.

*Matthew Henry*

Therefore, since we have
been justified through faith,
we have peace with God
through our Lord
Jesus Christ.

*Romans 5:1 NIV*

It is not the role of faith
to *question*, but to simply
*obey*. May the Lord grant
us the kind of faith that acts
"by faith, not by sight" . . .
for nothing is too
difficult for Him.

A. B. Simpson

Without faith it is impossible
to please God, because anyone
who comes to him must believe
that he exists and that
he rewards those who
earnestly seek him.

*Hebrews 11:6 NIV*

Genuine faith is believing and declaring what God has said, stepping out on thin air, and finding solid rock beneath your feet. Declare what God says you have. He will accomplish what you believe.

*L. B. Cowman*

Life has dimensions other
than those that can be
encompassed by the sense,
and into those dimensions
nothing can enter except the
principle of faith.

*G. Campbell Morgan*

You might as well shut
your eyes and look inside to
see whether you have sight,
as to look inside to discover
if you have faith.

*Hannah Whitall Smith*

Where there is faith
and a pure conscience,
there the Holy Spirit
certainly dwells.

*Martin Luther*

How many estimate difficulties in the light of their own resources, and thus attempt little and often fail in the little they attempt! All God's giants have been weak men, who did great things for God because they reckoned on his being with them.

*James Hudson Taylor*

Faith cannot be intellectually
defined; faith is the inborn
capacity to see God behind
everything, the wonder that
keeps you an eternal child. . . .
Beware always of losing
the wonder.

*Oswald Chambers*

Fear questions and retreats;

faith takes the things

God has promised

and moves forward. . . .

Fear says, "how?"

Faith says, "God!"

**Roy Lessin**

Just as the body without the spirit is dead, so also faith without works is dead.

*James 2:26 NASB*

All things are possible
to him who believes.

*Mark 9:23 NKJV*

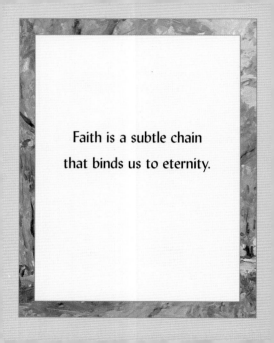

Faith is a subtle chain
that binds us to eternity.

Be of good comfort; thy faith
hath made thee whole.

*Matthew 9:22 KJV*

It is necessary that our feeble faith (lest it grow weary and fail) be sustained and kept by patient hope and expectation.

*John Calvin*

If you are absorbed in God,
you will be less eager to
please men, but you will please
them more.

*François Fenelon*

Christian faith is a grand cathedral, with divinely pictured windows.—Standing without, you can see no glory, nor can imagine any, but standing within every ray of light reveals a harmony of unspeakable splendors.

**Nathaniel Hawthorne**

The beginning of anxiety
is the end of faith, and the
beginning of true faith is
the end of anxiety.

*George Müller*

According to your faith

will it be done to you.

*Matthew 9:29 NIV*

This is the victory that
has overcome the world—
our faith.

*I John 5:4 NASB*

Man cannot live without faith
because the prime requisite
in life's adventure is courage,
and the sustenance
of courage is faith.

*Harry Emerson Fosdick*

The righteousness of God
is revealed from faith to faith;
as it is written, "The just
shall live by faith."

**Romans 1:17 NKJV**

It is good to have things settled by faith before they are unsettled by feeling.

Orthodoxy can be learned
from others; living faith
must be a matter of
personal experience.

*Buchsel*

He that builds his nest on a divine promise shall find that it abides and remains until he shall fly away to the land where promises are lost in fulfillments.

*Charles H. Spurgeon*

Faith sees the invisible,
believes the incredible,
and receives the impossible.

If we are faithless,

He remains faithful; for

He cannot deny himself.

*2 Timothy 2:13 NASB*

It takes leaps of faith to sense
the connections that are not
necessarily obvious.

*Matina Horner*

I'd rather walk in the dark
with God

Than go alone in the light;

I'd rather walk by faith
with Him,

Than go alone by sight.

Faith is the power of
putting self aside that God
may work unhindered.

*F. B. Meyer*

Feed your faith and doubt
will starve to death.

E. C. McKenzie

We are made partakers
of Christ, if we hold the
beginning of our confidence
steadfast unto the end.

*Hebrews 3:14 KJV*

Be strengthened with power
through His Spirit in the inner
man; so that Christ may dwell
in your hearts through faith.

*Ephesians 3:16-17 NASB*

Our circumstances
are irrelevant to the reality
of God.

A faith that can shine in
the darkness will know
no fear and feel no doubt.

The more we find God in
everything and every place,
and the more we look up to
Him in all our actions,
then the more we will conform
to His will, act according
to His wisdom, and imitate
His goodness.

**William Law**

The future holds
great things in store
for those who maintain
a steadfast faith.

Prayer gives strength
to the weak and faith
to the fearful.

Show me your faith without your works, and I will show you my faith by my works.

*James 2:18 NKJV*

The sincerity of a man's faith

is tested when his wallet

is challenged.

Faith is the starting-post
for obedience.

*Thomas Chalmers*

For we walk by faith,

not by sight.

*2 Corinthians 5:7 KJV*

It's not what men eat,
but what they digest that
makes them strong;

Not what we gain,
but what we save that
makes us rich, . . .

. . . Not what we read,
but what we remember
that makes us learned;

Not what we preach or pray,
but what we practice
and believe that makes
us Christians.

*Francis Bacon*

Faith is the bird that
feels the light and sings
to greet the dawn while
it is still dark.

*James S. Hewett*

Let us fix our eyes on Jesus, the author and perfecter of our faith, who for the joy set before him endured the cross, scorning its shame, and sat down at the right hand of the throne of God.

*Hebrews 12:2 NIV*

He is no fool
who gives what he
cannot keep to gain what
he cannot lose.

*Jim Elliot*

God may not take away
the darkness;

He may not take away
the pain;

But he has promised
us his presence

If we but trust,
and trust again.

For in our simple act
of trusting

We claim his pledge
of faithfulness;

Faith is strengthened,
our hearts uplifted,

When we believe
his way is best.

*Sarah Michaels*

When ye pray,

believe that ye receive them,

and ye shall have them.

*Mark 11:24 KJV*

Faith cometh by hearing,
and hearing by the word
of God.

*Romans 10:17 KJV*

I believe in the sun—

even when it does not shine;

I believe in love—

even when it is not shown;

I believe in God—

even when he does not speak.

**A Holocaust Victim**

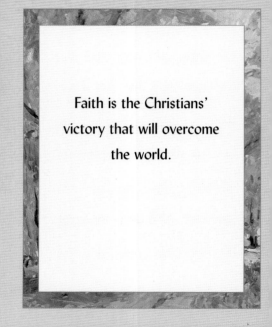

Faith is the Christians'
victory that will overcome
the world.

The dear child is glad of
all the Father's riches, and
the Father is gladder
of his dear child.

*W. Arnot*

Jesus answered
and said to them,
"Have faith in God."

*Mark 11:22 NKJV*

Men grow in stature only
as they daily rededicate
themselves to noble faith.

*Dwight D. Eisenhower*

Within you lives a power
greater than what lies
before you.

*Anonymous*

When you feel afraid,

seek the Father.

When you cannot see his face,

trust his heart.

If we walk faithfully in the way
God has marked out for us,
we will find God's presence
keeping us company.

Whenever God wants
to work in our lives,
he allows troubles to come
our way. If he wants to
bring us a miracle of faith,
he will send an impossibility.